GW01260572

hearty
chinese

hearty
chinese

Marshall Cavendish
Cuisine

Editor: Lydia Leong
Designer: Rachel Chen
Series Designer: Bernard Go Kwang Meng

This book contains previously published material from Flavours of the Middle Kingdom

Copyright © 2008 Marshall Cavendish International (Asia) Private Limited
Reprinted 2009

Published by Marshall Cavendish Cuisine
An imprint of Marshall Cavendish International
1 New Industrial Road, Singapore 536196

All rights reserved

No part of this publication may be reproduced, stored in a retrieval system or transmitted, in any form or
by any means, electronic, mechanical, photocopying, recording or otherwise, without the prior permission of the
copyright owner. Request for permission should be addressed to the Publisher, Marshall Cavendish International
(Asia) Private Limited, 1 New Industrial Road, Singapore 536196. Tel: (65) 6213 9300, Fax: (65) 6285 4871.
E-mail: genref@sg.marshallcavendish.com

Limits of Liability/Disclaimer of Warranty: The Author and Publisher of this book have used their best efforts
in preparing this book. The Publisher makes no representation or warranties with respect to the contents of this
book and is not responsible for the outcome of any recipe in this book. While the Publisher has reviewed each
recipe carefully, the reader may not always achieve the results desired due to variations in ingredients, cooking
temperatures and individual cooking abilities. The Publisher shall in no event be liable for any loss of profit or any
other commercial damage, including but not limited to special, incidental, consequential, or other damages.

Other Marshall Cavendish Offices:
Marshall Cavendish Ltd. 5th Floor, 32-38 Saffron Hill, London EC1N 8FH, UK • Marshall Cavendish Corporation.
99 White Plains Road, Tarrytown NY 10591-9001, USA • Marshall Cavendish International (Thailand) Co Ltd.
253 Asoke, 12th Flr, Sukhumvit 21 Road, Klongtoey Nua, Wattana, Bangkok 10110, Thailand • Marshall Cavendish
(Malaysia) Sdn Bhd, Times Subang, Lot 46, Subang Hi-Tech Industrial Park, Batu Tiga, 40000 Shah Alam, Selangor
Darul Ehsan, Malaysia

Marshall Cavendish is a trademark of Times Publishing Limited

National Library Board Singapore Cataloguing in Publication Data

Hearty Chinese. – Singapore : Marshall Cavendish Cuisine, c2008.
p. cm. – (Mini cookbooks)
"This book contains previously published material from Flavours of the Middle Kingdom"--T.p. verso.
ISBN-13 : 978-981-261-540-4
ISBN-10 : 981-261-540-7

1. Cookery, Chinese. I. Title: Flavours of the Middle Kingdom. II. Series: Mini cookbooks

TX724.5.C5
641.5951 -- dc22   OCN179727483

Printed in Singapore by Saik Wah Press Pte Ltd

contents

braised streaky pork Serves 4

This dish is traditionally enjoyed with the skin and fat, although increasingly, leaner cuts of meat are preferred by the health-conscious.

INGREDIENTS

Belly pork	450 g (1 lb)
Spring onions (scallions)	5, cut into 2.5-cm (1-in) lengths
Ginger	1.5-cm ($^3/_4$-in) knob, peeled and sliced
Chinese cooking wine (hua tiao)	2 tsp
Light soy sauce	2 tsp
Sugar	2 Tbsp
Preserved red bean curd	1 Tbsp, minced
Salt	1 tsp
Cooking oil	2 tsp
Green vegetables	150 g (5$^1/_3$ oz)
Sesame oil	1 tsp

METHOD

- Submerge pork in a pot of water and bring to the boil. Remove pork and rinse. Discard water. Place pork, spring onions, ginger, cooking wine, light soy sauce, sugar, preserved red bean curd and ½ tsp salt in a pot and add 500 ml (16 fl oz / 2 cups) water. Bring to the boil, then lower heat and simmer for 1 hour.

- Carefully remove pork and arrange in a heatproof bowl, skin side down. Drain sauce from pot into bowl with pork. Steam pork over high heat for 30 minutes.

- Meanwhile, heat oil in a wok and stir-fry green vegetables. Add remaining salt and sesame oil. Dish out onto a serving plate.

- Remove pork from steaming bowl and slice thickly. Arrange with cooked vegetables on serving plate. Reserve sauce.

- Heat sauce over high heat. Pour over pork and serve.

shredded pork with bamboo shoots Serves 4

This recipe specifies pork loin, a lean and tender cut of meat, which some may find rather dry.
Use a more fatty cut of meat, if desired.

INGREDIENTS

Bamboo shoots	150 g (5$^1/_3$ oz)
Chicken stock or water	500 ml (16 fl oz / 2 cups)
Cooking oil	3 Tbsp
Pork loin	200 g (7 oz), cut into long thin strips
Spring onion (scallion)	1, chopped
Ginger	1-cm ($^1/_2$-in) knob, peeled and shredded
Garlic	1 clove, peeled and sliced
Light soy sauce	1 Tbsp
Chinese cooking wine (*hua tiao*)	3 tsp
Salt	½ tsp
White vinegar	2 tsp
Corn flour (cornstarch)	1 tsp, mixed with 2 Tbsp water

NOTE
Ready-made chicken stock is available from supermarkets. To make your own, simmer 1 kg (2 lb 3 oz) chicken bones and parts in 3 litres (96 fl oz / 12 cups) water for 45 minutes, then leave to cool and skim off the layer of fat before using.

METHOD

• Place bamboo shoots and half the chicken stock or water in a pot and simmer for 20 minutes. Remove bamboo shoots and leave to cool slightly before shredding.

• Heat 1$^1/_2$ Tbsp cooking oil in a wok until just smoking. Stir-fry pork strips until lightly cooked, then add remaining oil while still stir-frying.

• Add spring onion, ginger, garlic and shredded bamboo shoots and mix well. Stir in light soy sauce, cooking wine, salt and vinegar and bring to the boil.

• Lower heat and stir in corn flour mixture to thicken sauce. Transfer to a serving plate and serve hot.

stir-fried pork Serves 4

Marinating the pork slices in a mixture of egg and corn flour helps coat the meat, giving it a smooth texture when cooked.

INGREDIENTS

Pork loin	300 g (11 oz), thinly sliced
Salt	$^1/_2$ tsp
Egg	1, beaten
Corn flour (cornstarch)	2 Tbsp, mixed with 8 Tbsp water
Chinese cooking wine (*hua tiao*)	1$^3/_4$ Tbsp
White vinegar	3 tsp
Light soy sauce	1$^1/_2$ Tbsp
Sugar	2 tsp
Cooking oil	250 ml (8 fl oz / 1 cup)
Spring onion (scallion)	1, chopped
Ginger	1-cm ($^1/_2$-in) knob, peeled and shredded
Garlic	1 clove, peeled and sliced

METHOD

- Place pork slices, salt, egg and two-thirds of the corn flour mixture in a bowl. Mix well and leave to marinate.

- In another bowl, prepare a sauce by combining cooking wine, vinegar, light soy sauce, sugar, 3 Tbsp water and remaining corn flour mixture. Set aside.

- Heat oil in a wok and slowly lower pork slices in one at a time. Deep-fry for 2 minutes or until golden brown. Remove pork slices and drain oil from wok.

- Return pork to wok and add spring onion, ginger, garlic and sauce. Stir-fry for a few minutes to heat and cook sauce. Garnish as desired and serve.

fried and steamed pork Serves 4

Steaming the pork helps it remain moist even after deep-frying.

INGREDIENTS

Streaky pork	500 g (1 lb 1$^1/_2$ oz), cut into 2.5-cm (1-in) cubes
Ginger	1.5-cm ($^3/_4$-in) knob, peeled and finely chopped
Salt	1 tsp
Egg	1, beaten
Corn flour (cornstarch)	100 g (3$^1/_2$ oz)
Cooking oil for deep-frying	
Chicken stock (page 13)	180 ml (6 fl oz / $^3/_4$ cup)
Light soy sauce	1$^1/_2$ Tbsp
Ground white pepper	1 tsp
Spring onions (scallions)	2, finely sliced

METHOD

• Place pork cubes in a bowl and cover with water. Leave to soak for 10 minutes, then drain well.

• Combine ginger, salt, egg and corn flour and coat pork cubes.

• Heat oil and deep-fry pork cubes until golden brown. Remove and drain well.

• In a heatproof bowl, combine fried pork with 4 Tbsp chicken stock and 1 Tbsp light soy sauce. Place in a steamer and steam for 1 hour. Carefully remove bowl from steamer and drain juices into a pan. Set aside.

• Turn bowl onto a serving plate and empty pork onto it. Set aside.

• Heat meat juices and stir in remaining chicken stock, light soy sauce and pepper. Bring to the boil, then lower heat to a simmer.

• Mix 1 tsp corn flour with 1 Tbsp water and stir into sauce to thicken it slightly. Pour sauce over pork cubes and garnish with spring onions.

deep-fried pouches Serves 4

These deep-fried pouches are very attractive and will also be adored by children. Replace the pork with minced chicken as a variation to this recipe.

INGREDIENTS

Minced pork	180 g (6^1/$_2$ oz)
Dried Chinese mushrooms	50 g (1^2/$_3$ oz), soaked to soften, stems discarded and finely diced
Chinese cooking wine (*hua tiao*)	1^1/$_2$ Tbsp
Salt	1 tsp
Sesame oil	1 tsp
Eggs	3, beaten
Corn flour (cornstarch)	3 Tbsp, mixed with 2^1/$_2$ Tbsp water
Plain (all-purpose) flour	3 Tbsp, mixed with 3 Tbsp water
Chinese ham	1 slice, cut into small dice
Spring onion (scallion)	1, finely cut
Cooking oil for deep-frying	

METHOD

- Combine minced pork and mushrooms in a bowl. Add cooking wine, ^{3}/$_4$ tsp salt and sesame oil. Mix well and shape into 2.5-cm (1-in) balls. Set aside.

- Combine eggs, remaining salt and corn flour mixture to make a batter. Heat a large nonstick pan until hot. Pour 1 Tbsp batter into the pan to make a pancake about 8-cm (3-in) in diameter. Remove and place on a plate to cool. Repeat with remaining batter.

- Place a ball of filling on each pancake and brush the edges with some flour mixture. Fold pancake in half to enclose filling. Brush with flour mixture and sprinkle with minced ham and spring onion.

- Heat oil for deep-frying and slowly lower pouches in one by one until crisp and golden brown. Drain and arrange on serving plates. Serve.

braised ox tail Serves 4

This Chinese version of braised ox tail is pleasantly spicy with the addition of Sichuan peppercorns and dried red chillies.

INGREDIENTS

Ox tail	1 kg (2 lb 3 oz), cut into 3-cm (1 1/2-in) lengths
Light soy sauce	3 Tbsp
Chinese cooking wine (*hua tiao*)	3 Tbsp
Salt	1 tsp
Cooking oil	500 ml (16 fl oz / 2 cups)
Spring onions (scallions)	2, chopped
Ginger	2.5-cm (1-in) knob, peeled and sliced
Sichuan peppercorns	1 tsp
Dried red chillies	3, soaked to soften, seeded and sliced
Sugar	1 Tbsp
Ground white pepper	3/4 tsp
Star anise	2
Chicken stock (page 13)	435 ml (14 fl oz / 1 3/4 cups)
Carrots	85 g (3 oz), peeled and thickly sliced
Bamboo shoot	85 g, (3 oz), thickly sliced

METHOD

- Marinate ox tail with 1 1/2 Tbsp light soy sauce, 1 Tbsp cooking wine and 1/2 tsp salt. Leave for 10 minutes. Heat oil in a wok and deep-fry ox tail until light red in colour. Remove and drain.

- Leave 2 Tbsp oil in wok and stir-fry spring onions and ginger. Add remaining soy sauce, cooking wine, salt, peppercorns, dried red chillies, sugar, pepper, star anise, chicken stock and ox tail. Cover and simmer for 2 hours.

- Remove ox tail and strain stewing liquid. Discard spices and herbs. Return ox tail to wok with strained stewing liquid. Add carrots and bamboo shoots and cook for another 8–10 minutes until carrots are tender. Dish out and serve.

hu-style mutton Serves 4–6

This is a dish of the Hu people, an ethnic minority in northwestern China.

INGREDIENTS

Stewing mutton	600 g (1 lb 5⅓ oz)
White peppercorns	1 tsp
Fennel seeds	1 tsp
Ginger	2.5-cm (1-in) knob, peeled and sliced
Spring onion (scallion)	1, cut into 2.5-cm (1-in) lengths
Salt	1 tsp
Ground white pepper	1 tsp
Dried wood ear fungus	15 g (½ oz), soaked to soften, shredded
Dried lily buds	10 g (⅓ oz), soaked to soften
Light soy sauce	1 Tbsp
Corn flour (cornstarch)	1½ Tbsp, mixed with 2 Tbsp water

METHOD

- Place mutton in a small pot and cover with water. Bring to the boil and cook for 30 minutes.

- Place peppercorns, fennel seeds and half the sliced ginger in a small muslin bag and secure. Add to boiling mutton stock. Cook for another 30 minutes until meat is almost done. Remove and leave to cool. Reserve mutton stock.

- Cut cooled mutton into strips. Combine mutton with remaining ginger, spring onion, salt, pepper and 4 Tbsp mutton stock in a heatproof bowl. Steam for 40 minutes. Drain stock from steamed mutton, then remove mutton to a serving plate. Set aside.

- Bring remaining mutton stock to the boil. Add wood ear fungus and lily buds. Stir in light soy sauce, then add corn flour mixture and stir to thicken sauce.

- Pour sauce over mutton and garnish as desired. Serve.

fragrant chicken Serves 4–6

Lightly simmered in marinade, then deep-fried, the chicken is not only moist, but extremely fragrant.

INGREDIENTS

Chicken	1, about 800 g (1 $^3/_4$ lb)
Spring onions (scallions)	2, chopped
Ginger	5-cm (2-in) knob, peeled and cut into chunks
Salt	1 tsp
Ground white pepper	1 tsp
Light soy sauce	3 Tbsp
Chinese cooking wine (*hua tiao*)	3 Tbsp
Sugar	1 Tbsp
Cooking oil for deep-frying	

METHOD

- In a pot, marinate chicken with spring onions, ginger, salt, $^3/_4$ tsp pepper, 1 $^1/_2$ Tbsp light soy sauce and 1 $^1/_2$ Tbsp cooking wine. Leave for 10 minutes before adding remaining pepper, light soy sauce, cooking wine and 1 Tbsp water.

- Place pot over low heat and simmer for 30 minutes. Remove chicken and drain. Pat chicken dry. Discard contents of pot.

- Heat oil in a wok and slowly lower in chicken. Continuously scoop oil over chicken until skin is crisp and golden brown. Remove and drain well. Leave chicken to cool.

- When chicken is cool, cut into bite-size pieces. Garnish as desired and serve.

chicken parcel Serves 4

This makes a good alternative to chicken nuggets and will be a hit with children. Omit the spring onion and ginger, if desired.

INGREDIENTS

Minced chicken breast	300 g (11 oz)
Spring onion (scallion)	1, finely chopped
Ginger	1.5-cm ($^3/_4$-in) knob, peeled and finely chopped
Egg	1, lightly beaten
Salt	$^3/_4$ tsp
Chinese cooking wine (*hua tiao*)	3 tsp
Dried bean curd skin	1 sheet
Egg whites	4
Corn flour (cornstarch)	50 g (1$^2/_3$ oz)
Cooking oil for deep-frying	

METHOD

- Combine minced chicken with spring onion, ginger, half the egg, salt and cooking wine.

- Brush remaining egg over bean curd skin and spoon minced chicken over. Bring edges of bean curd skin up to enclose filling and fold into a rectangular parcel. Cut away any excess skin. Flatten parcel by pressing down with a chopping board.

- Place parcel in a steamer and steam for 15 minutes over high heat. Remove and leave to cool.

- Beat egg whites until light and fluffy. Stir in corn flour to make a thick paste. Brush over steamed parcel.

- Heat oil and deep-fry parcel until golden. Drain well, then slice and place on a serving plate. Garnish as desired and serve.

tea-smoked chicken Serves 4–6

The smoke from the tea leaves and brown sugar adds a lovely, distinctive fragrance to the chicken.

INGREDIENTS

Chicken stock (page 13)	1 litre (32 fl oz / 4 cups)
Chicken	1, about 1 kg (2 lb 3 oz)
Cooking oil	4 Tbsp
Chinese tea leaves	85 g (3 oz)
Brown sugar	150 g (5$^1/_3$ oz)
Sesame oil	1 tsp

METHOD

- Heat stock in a large pot. Add chicken and cook for 20 minutes. Remove chicken and drain well. Reserve stock.

- Heat oil in a wok and stir-fry tea leaves until fragrant. Add brown sugar and stir-fry until smoke appears. The smoke will be yellowish in colour. Pour tea leaf mixture onto a sheet of aluminium foil, then place in a large, deep wok.

- Place a steaming rack over tea leaves and sit chicken on rack. Cover wok tightly and heat for a few minutes to smoke chicken.

- Remove wok from heat and leave chicken, covered, in wok for another 5 minutes. The chicken is ready when it turns a light brown colour. Slice chicken and arrange on a serving plate.

- Combine 5 Tbsp stock, 3 Tbsp water and sesame oil to make a sauce. Drizzle over chicken, garnish as desired and serve.

tender chicken Serves 4

This simple stir-fry is quick-to-do, and perfect for a simple weekday meal. Serve with steamed white rice.

INGREDIENTS

Chicken	1, about 800 g (1$^3/_4$ oz)
Cooking oil	4 Tbsp
Spring onions (scallions)	2, cut into 2.5-cm (1-in) lengths
Dried red chillies	5, soaked to soften, seeds removed and thinly sliced
Chinese cooking wine (*hua tiao*)	2 Tbsp
Salt	1 tsp
Ground white pepper	1 tsp
White vinegar	2 Tbsp
Water	125 ml (4 fl oz / $^1/_2$ cup)
Ginger	2.5-cm (1-in) knob, peeled and shredded
Corn flour (cornstarch)	1 Tbsp, mixed with 2 Tbsp water

METHOD

• Bring a large pot of water to the boil. Add chicken and cook for about 8 minutes. Carefully remove chicken and leave to cool slightly. Debone chicken and cut meat into bite-size pieces.

• Heat oil in a wok and stir-fry chicken strips, spring onions and dried red chillies for about 3 minutes.

• Add cooking wine, salt, pepper, vinegar and water. Stir and bring to the boil, then lower heat and simmer for 3 minutes. Add ginger.

• Stir in corn flour mixture to thicken sauce, then dish out and serve.

soy sauce chicken Serves 4

This dish is traditionally cooked in a clay pot, but if one is not available, any stewing pot with a lid can be used.

INGREDIENTS

Spring chicken	1, about 500 g (1 lb 1 1/2 oz), cut into small pieces
Cooking oil	90 ml (3 fl oz / 6 Tbsp)
Chinese cooking wine (*hua tiao*)	90 ml (3 fl oz / 6 Tbsp)
Light soy sauce	90 ml (3 fl oz / 6 Tbsp)
Spring onions (scallions)	2, cut into 3-cm (1 1/2-in) lengths
Ginger	3-cm (1 1/2-in) knob, peeled and sliced
Water	500 ml (16 fl oz / 2 cups)

METHOD

• Bring a pot of water to the boil and lower chicken pieces in briefly. Remove chicken and discard water.

• Rinse chicken with cold water, then place in a clay pot. Add oil, cooking wine, light soy sauce, spring onions, ginger and water. Cover and simmer over low heat for 45 minutes.

• Remove spring onions and ginger before serving, if desired. Garnish and serve.

chicken with pear cubes Serves 4

Pears add a lovely, fruity fragrance and juicy bite to this dish.

INGREDIENTS

Chicken breast	280 g (10 oz), cut into 1.5-cm ($^3/_4$-in) cubes
Egg	1, small, beaten
Corn flour (cornstarch)	2$^1/_2$ Tbsp
Cooking oil	250 ml (8 fl oz / 1 cup)
Chinese pears	150 g (5$^1/_3$ oz), peeled, cored and cut into cubes
Spring onions (scallions)	2, sliced
Ginger	1.5-cm ($^3/_4$-in) knob, peeled and sliced
Chinese ham	3 slices, cut into small squares
Salt	$^1/_2$ tsp

METHOD

• Mix chicken cubes with egg and corn flour.

• Heat 2 Tbsp oil in a wok and stir-fry chicken cubes. Add pear cubes and stir-fry lightly. Remove from heat.

• In the same wok, stir-fry half the spring onions and ginger. Add ham and return chicken and pear to wok. Add salt.

• Remove from heat and garnish with remaining spring onions to serve.

chicken with yam Serves 4

This dish is enjoyed for the soft, floury texture of the yam. Replace yam with potato, if desired.

INGREDIENTS

Chicken breast	280 g (10 oz), cut into cubes
Salt	1 tsp
Egg	1, beaten
Corn flour (cornstarch)	4 Tbsp
Cooking oil for deep-frying	
Yam	180 g (6^1/$_2$ oz), peeled and cut into cubes
Light soy sauce	1 Tbsp
Spring onion (scallion)	1, cut into 2.5-cm (1-in) lengths
Ginger	2.5-cm (1-in) knob, peeled and sliced
Sugar	1 tsp
Star anise	2
Chinese cooking wine (*hua tiao*)	2 Tbsp
Water	150 ml (5 fl oz / 10 Tbsp)

No**T**E

Cut the chicken and yam into cubes of a similar size for better presentation.

METHOD

• Marinate chicken with ^{1}/$_2$ tsp salt, egg and 3 Tbsp corn flour. Heat oil in a wok and deep-fry chicken until golden brown. Drain and place in a steaming bowl.

• Reheat oil in wok and deep-fry yam until golden brown. Drain and place on top of chicken in bowl.

• Pour remaining salt, light soy sauce, spring onions, ginger, sugar, star anise, cooking wine and water over chicken and yam. Steam for 15–20 minutes until chicken is tender.

• Pour steaming juices from bowl into a clean wok and bring to the boil. Lower heat and simmer until slightly reduced, then thicken with remaining corn flour mixed first with 1 Tbsp water.

• Turn chicken and yam out onto a serving plate. Pour sauce over and serve.

chicken with prawn balls Serves 4–6

A highly fragrant dish prepared with Chinese cooking wine and rice wine.

INGREDIENTS

Chicken	1, about 1 kg (2 lb 3 oz)
Salt	1 1/2 tsp
Chinese cooking wine (*hua tiao*)	3 Tbsp
Spring onions (scallions)	2, chopped
Ginger	1.5-cm (3/4-in) knob, peeled and sliced
Prawns (shrimps)	100 g (3 1/2 oz), peeled and minced
Corn flour (cornstarch)	2 1/2 Tbsp
Egg whites	2
Dried Chinese mushrooms	6–8, soaked to soften, stems discarded
Cooking oil	3 Tbsp
Chinese ham	3 slices, shredded
Bamboo shoot	20 g (2/3 oz), shredded
Ground white pepper	1 tsp
Light soy sauce	2 tsp
Rice wine	3 Tbsp

METHOD

- Marinate chicken with ³/₄ tsp salt, 2 Tbsp cooking wine, spring onions and ginger and place in a steaming bowl. Set aside for 2 hours.

- Place chicken in a steamer and steam over high heat for 1 hour. Remove chicken from heat and cool slightly. Cut chicken into bite-size pieces and arrange on a serving plate.

- Combine minced prawns, ¹/₂ tsp salt, corn flour and egg whites. Mix well and shape into small balls. Steam together with mushrooms for 5 minutes. Arrange with chicken on a serving plate.

- Heat oil and stir-fry ham and bamboo shoot. Add pepper, soy sauce, rice wine, remaining salt and 3 Tbsp water. Bring to the boil, then stir in 1 tsp corn flour mixed first with ¹/₂ Tbsp water to thicken sauce. Pour over chicken, prawn balls and mushrooms.

- Garnish as desired and serve.

sichuan chicken Serves 4

Both the Sichuan peppercorns and dried chillies add to the heat of this dish. Avoid biting into the Sichuan peppercorns as they leave a numbing sensation on the tongue.

INGREDIENTS

Chicken breast	450 g (1 lb), cut into small cubes
Salt	1 tsp
Chinese cooking wine (*hua tiao*)	2 Tbsp
Spring onions (scallions)	2, finely sliced
Ginger	1-cm ($^1/_2$-in) knob, peeled and finely sliced
Cooking oil for deep-frying	
Sichuan peppercorns	4 tsp
Dried red chillies	4, soaked to soften and cut into 2.5-cm (1-in) lengths
Water	160 ml (5 fl oz)
Sugar	1 Tbsp

METHOD

• Mix chicken with $^1/_2$ tsp salt, 1 Tbsp cooking wine, spring onions and ginger. Leave to marinate for 10 minutes.

• Heat oil in a wok and deep-fry chicken until golden brown. Remove and drain. Set aside.

• Leaving 2 Tbsp oil in wok, fry peppercorns until aromatic. Add dried chillies, chicken, water, remaining salt and sugar. Simmer until sauce is reduced to about one-third.

• Dish out and serve.

stir-fried clam meat Serves 4

A dish of succulent clams that can be easily and quickly prepared. Do not overcook clams as they will be tough and chewy.

INGREDIENTS

Clams	1.5 kg (3 lb 4$^1/_2$ oz), shelled and washed
Salt	1 tsp
Chinese cooking wine (*hua tiao*)	1 Tbsp
Ginger	1-cm ($^1/_2$-in) knob, peeled and chopped
Cooking oil	75 ml (2$^1/_2$ fl oz / 5 Tbsp)
Spring onions (scallions)	2, sliced
Water chestnuts	50 g (1$^2/_3$ oz), peeled and sliced
Dried Chinese mushrooms	30 g (1 oz), soaked to soften, stems discarded and sliced
Ground white pepper	$^1/_2$ tsp
Water	3 Tbsp
Corn flour (cornstarch)	1 Tbsp, mixed with 2 Tbsp water

METHOD

• Marinate clams with $^1/_2$ tsp salt, cooking wine and ginger. Heat 2 Tbsp oil in a wok and stir-fry clams briskly for 2–3 minutes. Remove from heat.

• Add remaining oil to wok and heat. Stir-fry spring onions, water chestnuts and mushrooms. Sprinkle in pepper and remaining salt. Add water and stir, then bring to the boil.

• Add corn flour mixture to wok, stirring to thicken sauce. Add clams and toss briskly to mix well. Dish out and serve.

prawns on sizzling rice crusts Serves 4

When the hot prawn and chicken mixture is poured over the freshly fried rice crusts, a sizzling sound is produced, hence the name.

INGREDIENTS

Cooked rice	450 g (1 lb)
Prawns (shrimps)	180 g (6^1/$_2$ oz), peeled and deveined
Egg white	1
Corn flour (cornstarch)	1 Tbsp
Cooking oil	
Chicken	120 g (4^1/$_2$ oz), boiled and shredded
Water	250 ml (8 fl oz / 1 cup)
Salt	1 tsp
Sugar	3 tsp
Tomato sauce	2 Tbsp
Chinese cooking wine (hua tiao)	2 Tbsp
White vinegar	2 Tbsp

METHOD

• Press cooked rice into an oiled baking tray to form a 1-cm (^{1}/$_2$-in) thick layer. Bake in a preheated oven at 120°C (250°F) for 30–40 minutes until rice is dry and slightly crisp. Remove rice crust from tray and break into pieces. Set aside.

• Coat prawns with egg white and corn flour. Heat 2 Tbsp oil in a wok and stir-fry prawns for 3 minutes. Add shredded chicken, water, salt, sugar, tomato sauce, cooking wine and vinegar. Bring to the boil, then stir in 1 Tbsp corn flour mixed first with 2 Tbsp water to thicken sauce.

• Meanwhile, heat oil for deep-frying until very hot. Lower in rice crusts and fry until crisp. Remove with a slotted spoon.

• Place rice crusts on a serving plate and pour hot prawn and chicken mixture over at the table. Garnish as desired.

deep-fried fish _Serves 4_

This dish may look difficult to do, but it is really quite simple. Alternatively, use a fish fillet with skin and omit step one.

INGREDIENTS

Firm white-fleshed fish	1, large, about 700 g (1 1/2 lb)
Salt	1 1/2 tsp
Chinese cooking wine (_hua tiao_)	3 Tbsp
Egg	1, beaten
Corn flour (cornstarch)	6 Tbsp
Tomato sauce	4 Tbsp
Sugar	150 g (5 1/3 oz)
White vinegar	90 ml (3 fl oz / 6 Tbsp)
Water	250 ml (8 fl oz / 1 cup)
Spring onion (scallion)	1, finely sliced
Ginger	1-cm (1/2-in) knob, peeled, sliced
Prawns (shrimps)	50 g (1 2/3 oz), boiled, peeled, diced
Bamboo shoot	20 g (2/3 oz), cut into small cubes
Dried Chinese mushrooms	20 g, (2/3 oz) soaked to soften and diced
Green peas	20 g (2/3 oz)

METHOD

- Cut fish head off and set aside. Cut fish along spine until about 4 cm (1 1/2 in) from tail. Remove spine bone up until uncut tail portion. Spread open fish, flesh side up and carefully remove remaining bones. Score flesh with criss-cross cuts. Marinate with 1 tsp salt, 1 1/2 Tbsp cooking wine and egg. Leave for 20 minutes, then dust with corn flour.

- Prepare sauce. Combine tomato sauce, sugar, white vinegar, water, remaining salt and cooking wine. Set aside.

- Heat enough oil for deep-frying in a wok. Spread fish out flat, flesh side up, on a large percolated ladle. Slowly lower fish into oil. Deep-fry until crisp and golden brown. Remove and drain.

- Using the same oil, deep-fry fish head until golden brown. Remove and drain. Arrange fish and fish head on a serving plate.

- Leaving 3 Tbsp oil in the wok, stir-fry spring onion and ginger briefly until aromatic. Add prawns, bamboo shoot, mushrooms and green peas. Stir-fry briefly and add sauce. Bring to the boil and thicken with 1 Tbsp corn flour mixed first with 2 Tbsp water. Pour over fish and serve.

sweet sour fish Serves 4

Unlike other sweet sour fish dishes with a thick tomato-based sauce, this sauce is light without being too overpowering.

INGREDIENTS

Firm white-flesh fish	1, about 800 g (1 3/4 lb)
Light soy sauce	2 Tbsp
Chinese cooking wine (*hua tiao*)	1 Tbsp
Ginger	2.5-cm (1-in) knob, peeled and finely chopped
Sugar	3 Tbsp
Red vinegar	4 Tbsp
Corn flour (cornstarch)	1 Tbsp, mixed with 2 Tbsp water

METHOD

• Gut fish and cut into two along the spine. Rinse well.

• Bring some water to the boil in a wok and carefully place fish in, skin side up. Boil for 8 minutes until fish is just cooked.

• Discard half the water. Add light soy sauce, cooking wine, ginger and sugar. Simmer for 10 minutes.

• Remove fish and place on a serving plate, skin side up.

• Add vinegar to wok and stir. Add corn flour mixture to thicken sauce, and bring to the boil. Pour over fish. Garnish as desired and serve.

braised fish tails Serves 4–6

This light and tasty sauce goes well with the delicate fish. Ensure that there is enough sauce to go around.

INGREDIENTS

Cooking oil	3 Tbsp
Spring onions (scallions)	2, cut in half
Ginger	2.5-cm (1-in) knob, peeled and sliced
Firm white-flesh fish tails	2, about 1.2 kg (2 lb 10 oz) in total
Light soy sauce	2 Tbsp
Salt	1 tsp
Chinese cooking wine (*hua tiao*)	2 Tbsp
Sugar	3 Tbsp
Chicken stock (page 13)	250 ml (8 fl oz / 1 cup)
White vinegar	2 tsp
Ground white pepper	1 tsp
Corn flour (cornstarch)	1 Tbsp, mixed with 2 Tbsp water

METHOD

• Heat oil and stir-fry spring onions and ginger for a few minutes. Discard spring onions and ginger. Carefully lower fish tails into wok and fry for 3 minutes.

• Add light soy sauce, salt, cooking wine, sugar and stock. Lower heat and simmer for 5 minutes.

• Add vinegar and pepper, and continue to cook for another 3 minutes. Add corn flour mixture to thicken sauce. Remove fish tails and arrange on a serving plate.

• Garnish as desired and serve.

fish slices with pickled mustard leaves Serves 4

Pickled mustard leaves need to be soaked before cooking to remove excess salt. They add a delicious salty flavour to the sliced fish.

INGREDIENTS

White fish fillet	250 g (9 oz), sliced
Egg white	1, lightly beaten
Salt	$^1/_2$ tsp
Corn flour (cornstarch)	1$^1/_2$ Tbsp, mixed with 3 Tbsp water
Pickled mustard leaves	70 g (2$^1/_2$ oz), soaked in cold water
Cooking oil	
Bamboo shoot	50 g (1$^2/_3$ oz), thinly sliced
Chinese cooking wine (*hua tiao*)	1 Tbsp
Water	90 ml (3 fl oz / 6 Tbsp)

METHOD

- Marinate fish slices with egg white, salt and half the corn flour mixture.

- Drain mustard leaves and chop finely.

- Heat 3 Tbsp oil in a wok and lightly scald fish slices until cooked and white. Remove and set aside.

- Leaving about 1$^1/_2$ Tbsp oil in wok, stir-fry pickled mustard leaves and bamboo shoot for 1 minute.

- Add cooking wine, water and fish slices. Bring to the boil, then stir in remaining corn flour mixture to thicken sauce.

- Dish out and serve.

stir-fried fish slices Serves 4

The egg and corn flour marinade ensures that the fish remains tender and moist even after frying.

INGREDIENTS

Egg	1, small, beaten
Corn flour (cornstarch)	4 Tbsp, mixed with 6 Tbsp water
White fish fillet	250 g (9 oz), cut into even slices
Light soy sauce	1 tsp
White vinegar	2 Tbsp
Sugar	3 Tbsp
Chinese cooking wine (*hua tiao*)	1 Tbsp
Cooking oil for deep-frying	
Spring onion (scallion)	1, shredded
Ginger	1-cm ($^1/_2$-in) knob, peeled and shredded

METHOD

- Mix egg with two-thirds of corn flour mixture, then use to marinate fish. Set aside.

- Prepare sauce. Combine light soy sauce, vinegar, sugar, cooking wine and remaining corn flour mixture. Set aside.

- Heat oil and deep-fry fish slices until crisp. Remove and drain.

- Leaving 2 Tbsp oil in wok, stir-fry spring onion and ginger until fragrant. Add sauce and bring to the boil.

- Add fish slices and stir-fry briskly, being careful not to break fish up. Dish out and serve.

fish chips Serves 4

Although traditionally enjoyed as part of a Chinese meal, these fish chips also make great appetisers or finger foods.

INGREDIENTS

White fish fillet	250 g (9 oz), cut into even strips
Spring onion (scallion)	1, chopped
Ginger	1-cm ($^1/_2$-in) knob, peeled and chopped
Salt	1 tsp
Chinese cooking wine (*hua tiao*)	3 tsp
Ground white pepper	$^1/_2$ tsp
Sesame oil	1 tsp
Corn flour (cornstarch)	200 g (7 oz)
Cooking oil for deep-frying	
Sesame seeds	2 Tbsp

METHOD

• Marinate fish with spring onion, ginger, salt, cooking wine, pepper and sesame oil. Leave for 30 minutes.

• Dust marinated fish strips with corn flour.

• Heat oil in a wok and deep-fry fish slices until golden brown. Drain and sprinkle with sesame seeds before serving.

fish rolls Serves 4

This recipe offers an alternative to whole or sliced fish. The fish is thinly sliced, then used as an edible food wrapper.

INGREDIENTS

White fish fillet	300 g (11 oz), cut into long, thin strips
Salt	1 tsp
Chinese cooking wine (*hua tiao*)	1 Tbsp
Corn flour (cornstarch)	5 Tbsp
Chinese ham	50 g (1²/₃ oz), thinly sliced
Bamboo shoot	50 g (1²/₃ oz), thinly sliced
Ginger	2.5-cm (1-in) knob, peeled and thinly sliced
Spring onions (scallions)	3, cut into 4-cm (1¹/₂-in) lengths + 2, finely sliced
Cooking oil	2 Tbsp
Chicken stock (page 13)	125 ml (4 fl oz / ¹/₂ cup)
Ground white pepper	¹/₂ tsp
Corn flour (cornstarch)	1 Tbsp, mixed with 2 Tbsp water

METHOD

- Marinate fish slices with ¹/₂ tsp salt and 3 tsp cooking wine. Leave for about 5 minutes.

- Drain and dust fish slices with corn flour, then top each one with slices of ham, bamboo shoot, ginger and length of spring onion. Roll fish slices up around filling and steam for 5 minutes.

- Heat oil in a wok and stir-fry finely sliced spring onions until fragrant. Add chicken stock, pepper and remaining salt and wine. Stir in corn flour mixture to thicken, then pour over fish rolls to serve.

fried dough strips with prawns Serves 4

This dish was originally created to represent autumn. The fried dough strips represent the falling autumn leaves.

INGREDIENTS

Plain (all-purpose) flour	150 g (5^1/$_3$ oz)
Prawns (shrimps)	150 g (5^1/$_3$ oz)
Egg white	1
Corn flour (cornstarch)	1 Tbsp, mixed with 2 Tbsp water
Spring onion (scallion)	1, finely cut
Ginger	1-cm (^{1}/$_2$-in) knob, peeled and chopped
Garlic	1 clove, peeled and sliced
Dried Chinese mushrooms	20 g (^{2}/$_3$ oz), soaked to soften, stems discarded and sliced
Bamboo shoot	20 g, (^{2}/$_3$ oz) sliced
Salt	1 tsp
Chinese cooking wine (*hua tiao*)	2 tsp

METHOD

• Combine flour with a little water to get a soft, pliable dough. Roll dough out into a thin sheet and cut into leaf shapes.

• Heat enough oil for deep-frying in a wok and deep-fry dough shapes until lightly brown. Drain and set aside on a serving plate.

• Coat prawns with egg white and corn flour mixture. Reheat oil and deep-fry prawns until just cooked. Pawns will curl and change colour.

• Leaving 2 Tbsp oil in wok, stir-fry spring onion, ginger and garlic until fragrant. Add fried prawns, mushrooms, bamboo shoot, salt, cooking wine and 2 Tbsp water. Mix well and pour on top of fried dough pieces. Serve immediately.

spicy bean curd Serves 4

This recipe offers a tasty way to enjoy bean curd. Savour it with a steaming bowl of white rice.

INGREDIENTS

Cooking oil	75 ml (2¹/₂ fl oz / 5 Tbsp)
Minced beef	120 g (4¹/₂ oz)
Spicy bean paste	1¹/₂ Tbsp
Black bean paste	2 tsp
Chilli powder	1 tsp
Salt	1 tsp
Light soy sauce	2 tsp
Ginger	2.5-cm (1-in) knob, peeled and chopped
Garlic	2 cloves, peeled and finely cut
Soft bean curd	400 g (14¹/₃ oz), cut into cubes
Corn flour (cornstarch)	2 Tbsp, mixed with 2 Tbsp water
Spring onion (scallion)	1, sliced
Sichuan peppercorn oil	1 tsp

METHOD

• Heat oil in a wok and stir-fry minced beef, breaking beef up. Add spicy bean paste, black bean paste, chilli powder, salt, light soy sauce, ginger, garlic and bean curd. Sprinkle in some water and bring to the boil.

• Lower heat and simmer for another 5 minutes. Stir in corn flour mixture, being careful not to break up bean curd.

• Add spring onion, then sprinkle peppercorn oil over. Dish out and serve.

bean curd sandwich Serves 4

This recipe offers a novel way to use bean curd, to sandwich a pork and prawn filling. Serve as part of a Chinese meal.

INGREDIENTS

Cooking oil	
Spring onions (scallions)	2, finely cut
Ginger	2.5-cm (1-in) knob, peeled and chopped
Minced pork	120 g (4^1/$_2$ oz)
Prawns (shrimps)	70 g (2^1/$_2$ oz) peeled and minced
Chinese cooking wine (*hua tiao*)	2 tsp
Chicken stock (page 13)	200 ml (6^1/$_2$ fl oz)
Salt	1 tsp
Corn flour (cornstarch)	1 Tbsp, mixed with 2 Tbsp water
Firm bean curd	250 g (9 oz), cut into long rectangular pieces
Plain (all-purpose) flour	6 Tbsp
Egg whites	4, beaten and mixed with 3 Tbsp corn flour
Sugar	1 tsp
White vinegar	1 tsp

METHOD

- Heat 2 Tbsp oil in a wok and stir-fry spring onions and ginger until fragrant. Add minced pork and prawns and stir-fry until meat changes colour and is cooked.

- Add cooking wine and half the chicken stock, $1/2$ tsp salt and half the corn flour mixture. Mix well and bring to the boil. Allow sauce to thicken.

- Arrange half the bean curd slices on a serving plate. Place a spoonful of stir-fried ingredients on top of each bean curd slice and sandwich with remaining bean curd slices. Dust with flour and set aside.

- Using the same wok, heat enough oil for deep-frying. Coat bean curd sandwiches with egg white-corn flour paste. Deep-fry one at a time, until golden brown. Remove and drain. Arrange on a serving plate.

- Leaving 1 Tbsp oil in wok, add remaining chicken stock, salt, sugar and vinegar. Cook over low heat for 3 minutes, then thicken sauce with remaining corn flour mixture. Pour over bean curd sandwiches and serve.

stuffed vegetable stems Serves 4

This dish was said to have been created to hide the meat, so bystanders would think that the person eating was having a vegetarian meal!

INGREDIENTS

Salt	2 tsp
Bok choy	250 g (9 oz)
Corn flour (cornstarch)	3 Tbsp
Minced chicken	250 g (9 oz)
Chicken stock	250 ml (8 fl oz / 1 cup)
Egg white	1, beaten
Chinese cooking wine (*hua tiao*)	3 tsp
Chinese ham	1 slice, diced

METHOD

• Bring some water to the boil in a pot. Stir in 1 tsp salt and blanch bok choy for 45 seconds. Drain and coat stems with corn flour. Place on a plate.

• Mix minced chicken with 4 Tbsp chicken stock, then add egg white, $^1/_4$ tsp salt and 1 tsp cooking wine. Shape mixture into balls and press into hollow of vegetable stems. Sprinkle with ham and place on a steaming plate. Steam for 5 minutes until chicken is cooked.

• Bring remaining chicken stock to the boil. Add remaining salt and cooking wine, then thicken with 1 Tbsp corn flour mixed with 2 Tbsp water. Drizzle over vegetables and serve.

fried egg noodles Serves 4

A quick and simple one-dish meal that can be easily prepared. Replace the prawns with sliced pork, if desired.

INGREDIENTS

Flat egg noodles 500 g (1 lb 1 $^{1}/_{2}$ oz)
Prawns (shrimps) 120 g (4 $^{1}/_{2}$ oz), peeled
Corn flour
  (cornstarch) 2 Tbsp
Cooking oil 2 Tbsp
Dried Chinese
  mushrooms 50 g (1 $^{2}/_{3}$ oz), soaked to soften,
  stems
                discarded and sliced
Salt 1 tsp
Water 150 ml (5 fl oz / 10 Tbsp)
Oyster sauce 2 tsp
Sugar 1 tsp
Ground white
  pepper $^{3}/_{4}$ tsp
Light soy sauce 1 Tbsp
Chinese chives 30 g (1 oz), cut into short lengths

METHOD

• Bring a pot of water to the boil and blanch noodles briefly. Drain well.

• Coat prawns with corn flour. Heat oil in wok and stir-fry prawns for 1 minute. Add mushrooms, salt, water, oyster sauce, sugar, pepper and light soy sauce. Mix well and bring to the boil, then add noodles and simmer for 5 minutes.

• Add chives and toss well. Transfer to a serving plate and serve immediately.

spinach noodles in soup Serves 4

A recipe for making your own spinach noodles is provided here, but you may also use other types of store-bought noodles, if desired.

INGREDIENTS

Plain (all-purpose) flour	500 g (1 lb 1^1/$_2$ oz)
Salt	2 tsp
Spinach	150 g (5^1/$_3$ oz), stems discarded
Egg	1, beaten
Cooking oil	2 Tbsp
Spring onions (scallions)	2, shredded
Pork loin	180 g (6^1/$_2$ oz), cut into thin strips
Tomatoes	2, sliced
Chicken stock (page 13)	500 ml (16 fl oz / 2 cups)
Hardboiled quail eggs	8, peeled and halved

METHOD

- Combine half the flour, ^{1}/$_2$ tsp salt and enough water to make a soft dough. Cover with a damp cloth and leave for 20 minutes.

- Finely mince spinach leaves and sprinkle with ^{1}/$_2$ tsp salt. Squeeze spinach of its juice using a piece of muslin. Discard fibre. Add remaining flour and beaten egg to spinach juice. Knead into a green dough, adding more water if necessary. Cover with a damp cloth and leave for 20 minutes.

- Press plain and green dough together, then flatten into a thin sheet with a rolling pin. Fan-fold dough, then cut into thin noodles using a long knife. Cook noodles in boiling water for 5 minutes, then rinse in cold water and divide into serving bowls.

- Heat oil and stir-fry spring onions until fragrant. Add pork and season with remaining salt. Allow stock to come to the boil and ensure pork is well cooked. Ladle over noodles.

- Top noodles with tomatoes and quail eggs. Serve immediately.

chicken soup

Chock full of ingredients from chicken, to barley, ham and leafy green vegetables, this soup can
be served as a meal on its own.

INGREDIENTS

Chicken	1, about 600 g (1 lb 5¹/₃ oz)
Spring onions (scallions)	2, cut into short lengths
Ginger	2.5-cm (1-in) knob, peeled and sliced
Sichuan peppercorns	1 Tbsp
Chinese cooking wine (*hua tiao*)	3 Tbsp
Barley	120 g (4¹/₂ oz)
Dried Chinese mushrooms	30 g (1 oz), soaked to soften, stems discarded and thinly sliced
Bamboo shoot	30 g (1 oz), cut into thin strips
Chinese ham	30 g (1 oz), cut into thin strips
Leafy green vegetables	30 g (1 oz), thinly sliced
Salt	1 tsp
Ground white pepper	1 tsp
White vinegar	2 Tbsp

METHOD

- Bring a pot of water to the boil. Carefully place chicken in and allow water to return to the boil. Remove chicken and rinse. Discard water.

- Place spring onions, ginger and peppercorns into a small muslin bag to make a bouquet garni. Set aside.

- Place chicken, 1.5 litres (48 fl oz / 6 cups) water, 1 1/2 Tbsp cooking wine, barley and bouquet garni into a stockpot. Simmer over low heat for 2–3 hours until chicken and barley are tender. Remove chicken, leaving soup to simmer. When chicken is cool enough to handle, shred meat.

- Remove bouquet garni from soup and add shredded chicken, mushrooms, bamboo shoot, ham and vegetables. Add remaining cooking wine, salt and pepper. Bring to the boil, then stir in vinegar. Serve hot.

shredded bean curd soup Serves 4

This simple soup is served as part of a Chinese meal. Make the soup even more substantial by adding some leafy green vegetables, if desired.

INGREDIENTS

Chicken stock (page 13)	750 ml (24 fl oz / 3 cups)
Chicken breast	30 g (1 oz), boiled and shredded
Bamboo shoot	30 g (1 oz), cut into thin strips
Firm bean curd	300 g (11 oz), cut into thin strips
Salt	1 tsp
Light soy sauce	2 tsp
Ground white pepper	1 tsp
Chinese ham	2 slices, cut into thin strips
Small prawns (shrimps)	125 g (4$^1/_2$ oz), peeled
Bean sprouts	30 g (1 oz), tails plucked and discarded

METHOD

• Place chicken stock, chicken breast, bamboo shoot and firm bean curd into a pot and cook over low heat for 8 minutes.

• Add salt, light soy sauce and pepper, and cook for another 5 minutes. Add ham, prawns and bean sprouts. When prawns turn pink, remove from heat.

• Ladle soup into serving bowls and serve.

vegetable soup Serves 4

This soup is slightly different from other Chinese soups, as the vegetables are stir-fried before boiling in stock. This way, the soup has an additional 'wok-flavour'.

INGREDIENTS

Baking soda	$^1/_2$ tsp
Spinach or other tender green vegetable	500 g (1 lb 1$^1/_2$ oz), cut into 5-cm (2-in) lengths
Dried Chinese mushrooms	100 g (3$^1/_2$ oz), soaked to soften, stems discarded
Chicken stock (page 13)	500 ml (16 fl oz / 2 cups)
Salt	1 tsp
Cooking oil	2 Tbsp
Chinese ham	1 slice, diced

METHOD

- Bring a pot of water to the boil and stir in baking soda. Blanch vegetables briefly, then drain and rinse in cold water. Drain well and set aside.

- Place mushrooms with 100 ml (3$^1/_2$ fl oz) chicken stock and $^1/_2$ tsp salt in a steaming bowl. Steam for 20 minutes.

- Meanwhile, heat oil in a wok and stir-fry vegetables for about 3 minutes until vegetables are slightly wilted. Add remaining stock, salt and steamed mushrooms, and bring to the boil.

- Ladle soup into serving bowls and sprinkle ham over. Serve.

fish soup Serves 4

Instead of using sliced fish, this fish soup is made by mincing fish meat into a paste, then rolling it into a sheet and cutting into strips.

INGREDIENTS

White fish fillet	150 g (5^1/$_3$ oz), finely minced
Corn flour (cornstarch)	150 g (5^1/$_3$ oz)
Chicken breast	60 g (2 oz), boiled and shredded
Dried Chinese mushrooms	3, soaked to soften, stems discarded and thinly sliced
Chicken stock (page 13)	750 ml (24 fl oz / 3 cups)
Salt	1 tsp
Ground white pepper	1 tsp
Spring onion (scallion)	1, finely sliced

METHOD

• Divide minced fish into 2 portions and roll into balls. Dust with corn flour and roll balls out into thin sheets.

• Bring some water to the boil in a large pan and gently lower in sheets of fish paste. Boil for 5 minutes, then remove fish sheets and rinse with cold water. Cut into long, thin strips. Set aside.

• Bring chicken stock to the boil and add shredded chicken, mushrooms, fish strips, salt and pepper. Return to the boil, then ladle into soup bowls.

• Garnish with spring onion and serve.

weights and measures

Quantities for this book are given in Metric, Imperial and American (spoon and cup) measures. Standard spoon and cup measurements used are: 1 tsp = 5 ml, 1 Tbsp = 15 ml, 1 cup = 250 ml. All measures are level unless otherwise stated.

Liquid And Volume Measures

Metric	Imperial	American
5 ml	1/6 fl oz	1 teaspoon
10 ml	1/3 fl oz	1 dessertspoon
15 ml	1/2 fl oz	1 tablespoon
60 ml	2 fl oz	1/4 cup (4 tablespoons)
85 ml	2 1/2 fl oz	1/3 cup
90 ml	3 fl oz	3/8 cup (6 tablespoons)
125 ml	4 fl oz	1/2 cup
180 ml	6 fl oz	3/4 cup
250 ml	8 fl oz	1 cup
300 ml	10 fl oz (1/2 pint)	1 1/4 cups
375 ml	12 fl oz	1 1/2 cups
435 ml	14 fl oz	1 3/4 cups
500 ml	16 fl oz	2 cups
625 ml	20 fl oz (1 pint)	2 1/2 cups
750 ml	24 fl oz (1 1/5 pints)	3 cups
1 litre	32 fl oz (1 3/5 pints)	4 cups
1.25 litres	40 fl oz (2 pints)	5 cups
1.5 litres	48 fl oz (2 2/5 pints)	6 cups
2.5 litres	80 fl oz (4 pints)	10 cups

Dry Measures

Metric	Imperial
30 grams	1 ounce
45 grams	1 1/2 ounces
55 grams	2 ounces
70 grams	2 1/2 ounces
85 grams	3 ounces
100 grams	3 1/2 ounces
110 grams	4 ounces
125 grams	4 1/2 ounces
140 grams	5 ounces
280 grams	10 ounces
450 grams	16 ounces (1 pound)
500 grams	1 pound, 1 1/2 ounces
700 grams	1 1/2 pounds
800 grams	1 3/4 pounds
1 kilogram	2 pounds, 3 ounces
1.5 kilograms	3 pounds, 4 1/2 ounces
2 kilograms	4 pounds, 6 ounces

Oven Temperature

	°C	°F	Gas Regulo
Very slow	120	250	1
Slow	150	300	2
Moderately slow	160	325	3
Moderate	180	350	4
Moderately hot	190/200	375/400	5/6
Hot	210/220	410/425	6/7
Very hot	230	450	8
Super hot	250/290	475/550	9/10

Length

Metric	Imperial
0.5 cm	1/4 inch
1 cm	1/2 inch
1.5 cm	3/4 inch
2.5 cm	1 inch

Abbreviation

tsp	teaspoon
Tbsp	tablespoon
g	gram
kg	kilogram
ml	millilitre